first love//first death

mara luar

mara luar

First paperback edition September 2024

Book design by Ingram Spark

ISBN 979-8-218-50764-0 (paperback edition)

Printed and bound by Ingram Spark

first love//first death

for the people who fight to keep them alive and end up losing anyways

mara luar

table of contents

Preface

We were just kids, sophomores in high school, when I lost my first love to suicide. Ever since, I have been sifting through the emotions of never ending grief, guilt, and heartache regarding my role in it.

We met when we were 14, and I moved to a small rural town in northern Minnesota. There were about 20ish kids in our class and he quickly made me feel seen, heard, accepted, and loved. This was probably the first time in my life I had felt this.

As time progressed, our relationship became codependent and toxic. There were frequent suicidal threats and trauma bonding between the two of us. Every time we fought (which was often) his *I am going to kill myself* trumped all. I knew how much he was hurting, but so was I, and he seemed to use suicide solely as a manipulation tactic. He took everything from my life and taught me that I couldn't live without him, yet was always threatening a reality without his existence.

But, we were each others' first loves and didn't know any better. We thought love and death were one and the same. We trauma bonded through our suicidal ideation and general distate at the world. I stayed with him out of fear of losing him and he stripped everything away from my life until I had nothing if I wasn't with him. These awful cycles carried on until his last breath.

A week after he turned 16, he successfully ended his own life and he had completely changed the trajectory of my life. He was my first love, he was my first death, he was the first thing that I held onto that gave my life purpose and then I didn't know what to do with the hole inside me he left behind.

I worshiped and idolized him because his death made him perfect and untouchable. I decided to forget all the damage he had done to me... Everyone else seemed to. I think it was easier that way. I felt guilty. I felt like it was my fault and everyone wanted a scapegoat which just happened to be me, and eventually I started to believe them.

Honoring most of what I have written from ages 17-22, I have compiled this book as a result. I wrote this to heal; I wrote this to process; and most of all, I wrote this so the people who are blamed for their partner's actions/deaths/sticking around do not feel as alone.

mara luar

I.   when we met

confession//15 years old

i don't know what love is but you feel right

h//vignette

silly
smart
crystal blue eyes
a short temper
quick on ice skates
too hard on himself

first love//first death

nicotine
flowing through my bloodstream
pumping to my heart and head
giving me a rush
i cannot get enough of
addictive and irresistible
from the marlboro reds you smoke
i want to be held in your lips like them
i want you to inhale me until just the ashes are left

you will be the death of me
we will be the death of each other

modern day romance

my mornings were never good
until you wished me one everyday
at 6:50 am in a text message

i signed up for all the same classes as you

i hate getting out of bed
i hate going to school
the only thing that gets me through it is knowing
that i get to see you

butterfly kisses

i wish you could see yourself the way i see you
i tell you
you press your eye to mine
eyeball on eyeball
and say that *now you can*

secrets//toxic masculinity

you like me because i'm damaged
the sunlight creeps through the cracks in me
and you stare in fascination

you glow and glimmer you say
with a hint of jealousy
and that you wish that you could too
no
you don't say that last part but your eyes do

because you are the same as me
but different

i nod my head in silent acknowledgement
and know that we both are seeing the same guys in
our mind
shoving you into the tempered glass on the ice rink

overtime

both praying for our school's team to lose
just so we could go into overtime
and have more time to hold each others' hands

the first time you told me that you loved me

it was in a taco johns after an away game
our team lost and you blamed yourself
it was the first time i ever really saw you mad
and it broke my heart to see you that upset

but you mended my heart right back together by
confessing your love

the first time you ever told me you loved me was
right after the first time i had seen you mad
i should have known then that your anger and love
would go hand-in-hand

II.   before

bullying//trapped

they bully me when i am with you
but bully you when you're without me
i have no one but you
and we have no one but each other

my happiness was in your hands//selfless

you know my happiness is in your complete control
and you take joy in making me suffer because you
are suffering too

but i let it happen and surrender myself to you
because i am too afraid to lose you

i am too afraid of who i am without you
i am afraid i have nothing without you

toxic

spitting insults down my throat sugar coated with
sweet words and kisses
putting your cigarettes out on my skin
doting the other pretty girls
making me lay awake at night with my phone in
hand
wondering why i wasn't enough
slicing my skin as my eyes shed salty tears only to
have you laugh at them
the next time
we laid
naked

we made each other explode

don't smile, he said
you wear your rage so pretty

suicidal threats//trapped

you just know that someone like me
deserves better than you
and that this is the only way to keep me

diminishing spark//entitlement

with each day my spark dims
because i give it all away
to you
a gift to keep you happy
because your happiness is mine too

and i keep giving because i am nothing
no one
not needed
or cared for by anyone else
except you

you made sure of that

how many times are you going to kill me?

virginities gone with a following pregnancy scare
you acted as if it was the end of the world

it felt like it for me

two days later you say yes to prom with another girl
and then break up with me

i come back to school a week later
excited to see you

excited to show you that i am still alive
and i push through the murmuring and ignore the
gossip

my heart fills when i spot you and rush over
our friend says *look mara is back!*
you stare right through me and say
no she's not

we never let each other get the last word

i can't talk to you anymore and i don't want to

emergency room//you pushed me to the edge

i write my first name and last name
no
i wrote my first name and then yours

no more blind faith for empty promises

i always chose you
and you only ever choose yourself

promises//text sent 1.24.2016

when your heart stops beating
so will mine

first love//first death

34

you called it love//we only wanted death or each other

you fucking gave me panic attacks, landed me in a hospital, almost cost me my life, and dared to call it love

was it a lie?//why'd you leave me then?

you can't love someone as much as i love you and not the next day

cheating

we were still together
even when apart

you said *but she's not you*
and i say in defeat
she's not me

games

angry outbursts
fighting for no reason
you dangle suicide over my head
until i scream and cry
do you really hate me that much?
no
you really only hate yourself

ironic//you'd never have the chance

and then i realized you were never going to live up
to the person that i made you out to be...

antidepressants//the burden of keeping you alive

smuggled antidepressants
in my own name
i push into your palm
you laugh
and throw them into the snow
you're my antidepressant

i should have known

an inseparable twine connecting our hearts to each
other
you sharing your deafening suicidal thoughts
and fears of inadequacy
the bullying

everything that you once loved now only brings you
anger
more anger than what was already there

you've scared me for years but now
i am scared for you
and that place you must stay
living in your head

i said
either i am saving your life
or teaching you a lesson

-the boy who cried wolf//the wolf did come

mara luar

III.   right before

text pt 1

everyone is out to get me

text pt 2//a win before a loss

it's your fault i'm not dead yet

mara luar

IV.   february 16, 2017

V.　after

denial

this cannot be possible
if you really did die
then a piece of me has too
and i am not ready to accept that

stealing my thunder

it was supposed to be me in the casket
not you you asshole

after

i've always been an angry person
but when you died
that anger calcified into rage
at the world
and whoever/whatever god is

the funeral dress//he was 76 you were 16

i saw a black dress at a thrift store and bought it
preparing for my ill grandpa's death
i never imagined i would be wearing it to your
funeral first

mara luar

i died too

your one finite death punishes me
killing me over and
over and over
again years later

i died too that day
and no one noticed because i wasn't the one in the
casket...

two months since you left this world

abandoned me and your hope
sent a bullet through your head that continued
straight through my heart

you
dead and gone
me
a survivor
having to deal with the pain for the rest of my life

patch up the hole in my heart
but still deal with the ghosts of our past that haunt
me
and your ghost too
alone

i don't know how to live without you
i don't know if i can
i don't know if i want to

building new memories

it feels wrong to be here
doing the same things that we loved to do together
without you

in the ditch//tired of unwanted explanations

i crashed my car into the ditch
your friend rescued me

and he said it was you that made me crash
and that you were trying to bring us together

reminders//ptsd

a fume fills my nostrils
creeping through my nose and up to my head
like a plague spreading triggers of our memories
agony and pain from a smell
that once brought me comfort

.

did you know??//are you watching us??

consoling me
at your headstone
he tries to kiss me
and says it would be what you want
who you thought was your best friend

your other best friend
takes me to prom
in the car that would have been yours

another one tries to sleep with me
was it to get back at you
for always shining brighter than him
or was it to feel closer to you

*people grieve in strange ways desperately trying
to cling onto the little pieces left behind*

regrets//what he says

you should have never taken that plan b
he might have still been alive if you didn't
at least we'd have your kid if he still ended his life

consolation and consumption

just fifteen
my head is limp on your lap and tears stream down
my face
liquor on my breath and tears blurring my eyes
i want to be dead
i ask why i'm not

*because mara, god doesn't want you yet. you're
meant to still be here*

but now... i cry
i cry not only because of this, but because of you
why was god ready to take you, but not me?
why had i squirmed out of death's grasp
and the first time you tease death it steals you away

you did everything in your power to make my bad
thoughts go away, and i tried to help you,
but i wasn't enough

i couldn't save you, god couldn't even bare the
decency to fucking save you

the guilt consumes me

it's time to get out of bed and change your clothes

life goes on
with
or
without
You

forever 16

it's been 3 years since the darkness swallowed you
i'd like to forget and move on but i can't
day-to-day activities sting...
wondering if you'd be with me if you were still
here

sometimes my heart sings but then
then that darkness creeps
trying to swallow me like it did
you

i want to forget
i want to move on
but the aftermath of what you did
comes back to haunt me
every single day

sometimes i wonder which one of us is
really dead

i am a new person now

you'd hate who i am now
i'm glad you're not alive to see it

my mom is worried//you're just a boy

she told me to stop idolizing you
just because you're dead doesn't mean you are
perfect

she reminds me of all the things you put me
through
she reminds me of how mean you were
and how i was so hurt and small and broken with
you

she reassures me that if you were still alive, we
would still be fighting and you'd be pissing me off
on the daily

no one else seems to remember though
and i want to forget all the bad too

you are not an angel, you were just a boy

guilt//milestones

time passes and i do all the things that you never
got the chance to do
i get my driver's license
and blast the songs that we listened to together
i go to prom with your best friend
and your grandparents let us take what would have
been your car
i graduate high school and go to college
and go to hockey games that you should have been
playing in
if you were still alive

i celebrate all your birthdays without you
and as i age you stay forever young
with each new memory i make
our memories together fade
further away

what do I hold onto now that you are gone

and i feel guilty
and it feels wrong
with each passing year you grow further and further
away and my life gets bigger and bigger
and your's
your life
fades to nothing
just an echo down the hallway

suicide loss survivors grief and guilt

guilt is an additional stage of grief that suicide
survivors must go through
all the what ifs
and should haves
those questions that torment your soul and keep
you awake late into the night
it hurts to think that things could have been
different
and even harder to think about how things would
be different now

if they had just chosen to stay

doubts

he is in a better place now
yes he is
because he is no longer with me

enablers//identity

after his death i was a ticking time bomb that
everyone was terrified would explode at any
moment

reminders//i am not as fragile as you think

a song that mentions suicide
a tv show where someone dies
a joke
less loud over time
sometimes the reference slips your mind
but then
a frantic apology and subject change
it did not trigger me until you reminded me of how
fragile i really am

the curse of being a teenage girl with a suicidal boyfriend

an explanation
all the eyes trying to pry apart
a why
no... not a *why*
but a *who*

last night's dream

long eyelashes
and pretty crystal blue eyes

i wish i could bring you back to life like i somehow
did in my dream tonight

expectations

sometimes giving up completely seems easier than
disappointing others
i don't blame you

where were you?

there was no light
there was no release
just the absence of living
darkness

not dead, but not alive either

elysian fields

not dead, but not really alive either
i loiter the realm between the two
comatose and numb
simultaneously over-ambitious and paralyzed
i can smell the rot and feel myself decaying
how do i live?
when my whole life is centered around death?

but you can't

your mother wished me a happy birthday

dead inside

you're dead and i am not
but what's the use
i might as well be and quite frankly
it feels like i am already

life feels empty and hollow without you
i don't know how to fill the hole that you left in my
life when you left

days are monotonous and blur together
the questions about your death
and my own self doubts in the role i played
haunt me

doubts

i feel like i disappointed you
like i wasn't all that you needed
that i didn't love you enough and could have
stopped this nightmare

i am usually good at pushing those thoughts away
but there is always that part deep inside me that
wonders if they were right
if i really didn't love you enough
if i left you in a whirlwind you could never get out of

is it my fault you are dead?
if i did things differently would you still be alive?
was it all doomed from the start?

a tip

don't give the people you love a special text tone
when they die whenever you hear it on someone
else's phone
you will relive every single moment again

expiration date pt 1

would i still choose you if i knew our love had an
expiration date?
yes
in every lifetime

expiration date pt 2

despite your death
there is no expiration date
on all the grief i carry for you
the pain from what you did
and my love for you

mara luar

VI.   **finding love again**

nostalgia is so comfortable

will i forever be chasing ghosts of the past?
constantly in a state of grief
mourning for who i was and who you were
and comparing every love to ours?

**please don't leave me on read for too long if i
love you**

everytime you don't answer me
my brain prepares me for the worst
a car crash
a gunshot
you gone
and me having to relive it all again

mara luar

lukewarm//conditional value

i can't do lukewarm love
i don't want it unless it's scalding my skin
and i am drowning in it
and unless it hurts me
it doesn't feel real

when i love it is relapse
because i am eager to sacrifice every single part of
myself
to whoever i am with

misconceptions

love either kills you or they die first

restless//am i too dark for you?

the late nights i couldn't tolerate
alone in our bed
with no word from you or clue where you were

maybe the girl w the crocheted hat
the one who dances and i catch you smiling at
or the one who sings sunshine
while i only sing darkness
and cry and shout and drink wine

i thought it would be different
i thought you were better than him
but late into the night i still lay awake,
anxious about not being enough

what the new one said

i am here and i am alive...
it is impossible to compete with the dead

i don't want to love you anymore

do we have a choice of who we love?
i think to some capacity we do
we attract and accept what we think we deserve
maybe that is why all my lovers end up being the
same

no matter how long the love bombing or
honeymooning goes on or how different i think that
this time around is...
the manipulation and abuse remains
sometimes covert but now mostly overt

since we have a choice of who we love
we must love ourselves first

this is the **only** way to go into a healthy and sound
relationship

my grief swallowed you

the end
of a rocky relationship
angry words exchanged
trying to see who can stab the deepest

you say
it felt like you a loved someone dead more than me
who is here and living

but he was my first love...
a pit in my stomach
a hole of unresolved grief
that was compartmentalized and put away when i
met you
or at least i thought

i'm sorry

redefining love

i've heard about the love you'd kill for
the love you'd die for
i've felt it
i know it's real and exhilarating
but what about the other kind of love?
the scary kind
the kind of love that makes you want to live?
when all you ever known love to be is the ultimate
sacrifice

a quiet thought

sometimes a quiet thought tells me
that you had to die
in order for me to grow

angel

what they need to understand
is that i will always compare
them to the angel in my mind
and i cannot help it

possession//possessed

when we fight and argue
i hate who i become

i grow fangs and bite
and scream and growl
like a scared dog

i want to blame it on him
but i become him
trying to prevent the same situation happening
again now with you

i am tired of being the one who gets hurt in the end
and i am tired of being the one who hurts the other
in the end

this is not romeo and juliet

how do i reteach my traumatized brain into
thinking that killing yourself is not the most
romantic gesture of all

unsafe

you taught me how it was to feel safe for the first
time in my life
and then took it all away

you killed the child in me who just simply wanted
love from you
but that was too much to ask...

the living

i know how to grieve the dead but no one ever
warned me how much harder it would be to grieve
the living

the glue//you cannot take my pain away

when we found each other i was broken
all the others had promised me sunshine and
healing
frantically trying to put my pieces back together

but he just smiled and held my hands and told me
that i was beautiful

first love//first death

Acknowledgement

In the midst of the 2014 Tumblr epidemic, where black and white gifs filled my feed, mental illness was romanticized, and we all idolized Lana Del Rey, I was a victim and pursour of all sorts totally infatuated with this aesthetic heterotopia, and from this you can hear and see heavy influence on my prose and art choices. A controversial ode, but one I must acknowledge to honor who I was back then and the creation of my book.

Wrapped up in a lack of identity as a mentally ill teenager, where the small town generational norms of gender roles were exasperated, I felt I had found a new purpose associated with my identity—to exist for him, saitate him, and help him. His needs were mine, and if he wasn't doing good then neither was I.

This leads to my next acknowledgement: all the people who take the responsibility of the men in their lives. It was a subconscious role I played because it did feed into my self-image and purpose, and in a patriarchal society we are conditioned to it time and time again. We are expected to patrol, regulate, feel, and pick up the pieces of the men in our lives and then receive all the shame, guilt, and blame when those same men fail. This is for you.

Leading up to the publishing of this book, I created a small Instagram page, @maraluarwrites, and received so much support from people who had experienced similar situations or feared one unraveling. It is more common than most know, yet being in it can be so isolating. So many partners feel the obligation to literally take the weight of their partners' lives upon their shoulders. They are either manipulated into it, conditioned to it, severe empaths (like me), or a mix of all of those things. This is not fair, or how it should be, and it is never their responsibility in the first place. I want to acknowledge all of you on my online platforms as well for creating and contributing to a space where we can be vulnerable and talk about these things.

Next, I'd like to thank my family.

My dad, Doug, who as a stranger, in his ex-wife's hometown, brought me to my partner's funeral full of generations of people who knew each other grieving a teen suicide... *Yikes.*

Then, to my fairy godmother, or stepmom, Stephanie, who was the first person to really teach me how to advocate for myself as a kid who no one took seriously.

Thank you to my sisters, Zoë and Odessa, who have listened to my trauma jokes since they were young and kept secrets from my mother while I was hurting.

Thank you to my mother, Sheri, who has always nurtured and encouraged the writer in me. Without her, I wouldn't be the reader or writer that I am today. I wouldn't ask for any other mom.

With my mother being an educator, this leads me to acknowledge all the educators in my life who have encouraged and helped me grow. They are the backbone of our society and should really be thanked and paid more.

My professor, Brandy Lindquist, who was the first professor to allow me the space to grieve and heal through my writing. Next, a feminist badass with a PhD, Dr. Wright, who pushed and challenged the limits of any academic writing I had ever done. And finally, Mrs. Carlson, my high school art teacher, who allowed me to use supplies, do independent projects, and spend time in her art classroom when I was bullied and outcast from the others in my grade.

Thank you to the two professionals that have helped most with my mental health: Lindsey and Luke. Lindsey has been there for me through thick and thin, spanning longer than any other professional, and then my therapist, Luke, who has helped me challenge and redefine my negative core beliefs surrounding my value and worth that have afflicted me for as long as I can remember.

Next, I'd like to acknowledge my anchors and closest friends: Liv, Rachel, Giiwedin, and Peyton, who let me run my mouth dry until things don't hurt as much anymore. They dance, laugh, and cry with me. They have been my #1 cheerleaders in the process of making this book a reality.

I must also acknowledge past lovers who have loved me and tried to support me despite all of this. It is definitely no easy thing to do to be with someone whose trauma and idolization of a dead ex seeps into the current day.

Thank you to my lost one's family and friends who have included me in their grief journeys as well and try to keep his spirit alive with me.

Thank you to anyone else who has been a part of my grief journey and who has shown me love and support while I have been hurting and healing.

And finally, whether my book speaks to one person or thousands, I want to acknowledge you, reader, holding this book right now. Thank you for listening and sharing this moment with me. Your life matters.

Fly high, H <3

About the Author:

Mara Luar, 23 years old and with a degree in Professional Writing, has always relied on writing to be the one constant in a life full of change and chaos.

Mara Luar spent their early childhood nestled on the Idaho side of the Grand Tetons. When the recession of 2008 hit, Mara Luar moved to a Hudson River town called Nyack, a little north of New York City, with family.

Spending summers in rural Minnesota since a kid, Mara eventually left the busyness of New York and moved to Minnesota. Mara Luar has lived in Lake of the Woods, Breezy Point, and now Duluth.

Mara Luar enjoys brewing and sipping tea, reading/writing, dive bar karaoke, lifting weights, live music, and doing anything outdoors.

first love//first death is Mara Luar's debut poetry collection surrounding the experience of losing their first love to suicide at 17 years old.

 @maraluarwrites